Medicine is Not a Job!

The Secret Every Physician and Physician-Hopeful Should Know

JN Olayiwola, MD, MPH, FAAFP

Copyright © 2014 JN Olayiwola, MD, MPH, FAAFP

All rights reserved.

ISBN: 0692270418
ISBN-13: 978-0692270417 (Jacqueline Nwando Olayiwola)

Are you a high school student contemplating a career in medicine? A college student or postbaccalaureate following the pre-med path? A resident physician thinking about next steps? A practicing physician challenged by the realities of your work? This book is meant for you.

Medicine is Not a Job is the written version of a highly acclaimed speech Dr. Olayiwola gave to 250 high school students interested in careers in medicine in 2014.

The book delves into some of the inspiration and motivation behind becoming and continuing as a physician and understanding the difference between a job and a calling. With concise real life examples, any physician or physician-hopeful can surely draw motivation.

DEDICATION

This book is dedicated to my husband Paul, who supports me continuously; my children, Darius and Nissi, who challenge and motivate me regularly; my parents, who encourage me constantly; my three natural siblings, my two "adopted" Indian and Ghanaian siblings, and their families, who continue to amaze me with their inspiration, intellect and humor.

CONTENTS

	Acknowledgements	i
1	The Secret	1
2	The Early Days	3
3	Who is this Woman?	5
4	The Roots	8
5	The Branches and Fruit	10
6	Reason Number 5	12
7	Reason Number 4	16
8	Reason Number 3	20
9	Reason Number 2	24
10	Reason Number 1	30
11	What's the Point?	35
12	And Finally!	38

ACKNOWLEDGEMENTS

On July 7, 2014, I gave a keynote speech for the National Youth Leadership Forum (NYLF), through the larger Envision network, at University of California, Berkeley. NYLF and Envision provide incredible leadership and exposure to students all over the States as they pursue professional careers.

For weeks leading to the event, I pondered over how to deliver a speech that was both inspirational and pragmatic for 250 high school students from all over the country who were interested in medicine.

Though it was a gamble, I chose to expose some of the hard truths about being a physician, but couched in the fact that this profession is still very doable and gratifying if one is truly called to it. And the gamble worked! After my speech, both students and NYLF/Envision staff shared excitement and even encouraged me to transform my speech into a book that more students could read.

I cannot thank those wonderful students and NYLF/Envision staff enough for their faith in my words and their inspiration to spread them!

1
THE SECRET

If you have decided to buy, or better yet, to read, this book, I understand that you are interested in a career in medicine and are looking for the secret in getting there. Kudos and yippee! You are inquisitive and curious. Bravo! But, I want you to keep reading. If you are a doctor already, you will understand where I am coming from, even if you did not realize it. If you are a student or a physician-hopeful, the revelations in this book may surprise you.

For the students reading my book, I remember being in your position many, many, many years ago, and contemplating my strategy to become a doctor and get a job in medicine. This strategy was designed and executed over a number of years, honestly starting back from my high school days, way before I knew an important secret in medicine, which I will soon disclose.

2
THE EARLY DAYS

I worked very hard as a high school student, like those of you in high school are doing now. I was on this quest towards medicine and knew that all of the essential ingredients had to be included for my recipe to be perfected. I worked even harder in college, putting in hours of class and marathon study, completing my first degree in three years, and inching closer to that goal.

However, I hate to break this to you, but no matter how hard you work, you are NOT going to get a job in medicine, because medicine is not a job!

This must sound awful right? No one has told you this yet correct? It's a sad revelation and I hope your parents and teachers don't get upset with me for telling you this secret, but medicine is not a job. Before you go trying to get a refund for this purchase, please read on – just continue – you have a goal right?

Medicine is not a job!

3
WHO IS THIS WOMAN?

By now, you are wondering who I am and why I have the guts and gumption to say this to you. And I am sure you are wondering why a jobless person would take the time to share this insight, instead of looking for a job!

My name is Dr. Nwando Olayiwola, and I am a practicing family physician, the Associate Director of the Center for Excellence in Primary Care, and an Assistant Professor of Family and Community Medicine at University of California, San Francisco (UCSF). I am also a wife and a mother of two lovely children.

My current role involves working at the San Francisco General Hospital's Family Health Center and taking care of some of the most underserved, vulnerable and sick patients in the San Francisco Bay Area; doing practical work and research to improve the way we deliver that care, and teaching UCSF medical students and residents as they journey through their medical education towards that reality of not getting a job.

My work has changed and improved the health of thousands of people across the United States and I am working to leave a larger imprint in the global community. I have worked hard to get to where I am, and I had every reason to do so.

I am the first daughter and second child of Nigerian immigrants who came to this country after a divisive civil war that tore the country apart, seeking education and peace at the same time.

...child of Nigerian immigrants...

My parents raised four children in America to become an Air Force pilot, physician and attorney (my older brother), a physician and public health professional (me), a social worker and attorney (my younger sister), and another attorney, entertainer and musician (my youngest brother).

4
THE ROOTS

From a very early age, the values of hard work, determination, focus, perseverance and excellence were instilled in all of us. With parents who were both doctoral trained professionals, our father being a professor of Political Science and our mother a systems engineer, we had no choice but to excel.

...hard work, determination, focus, perseverance and excellence...

I grew up in Columbus, OH where I went to high school, and where, like you, I systematically engaged myself in all I could to pursue a career in medicine. I applaud you for having the vision now and for taking advantage of the opportunities that will get you to where you want to go.

After high school, I went to college at The Ohio State University and then medical school at The Ohio State University/Cleveland Clinic Foundation.

By the time I finished medical school, I was intensely drawn not only to improving the health of the underserved patients I would take care of, but improving the health of their communities. I was inspired by the thought of being a doctor that cared for urban, underserved, poor and minority communities, so I went to do my family medicine residency at Columbia University/New York Presbyterian Hospital in Washington Heights, New York, NY, which was an immersion experience indeed!

5

THE BRANCHES AND THE FRUIT

During my three years at Columbia/New York Presbyterian Hospital, I learned so much about the skill and art of medicine, had some of the best mentors, understood so much more about patient care and being a wise and compassionate doctor, formed a non-profit that provided HIV/AIDS education and prevention to minority adolescent females in high risk areas, and learned that many of my professional interests were aligned with public health.

After this, I was selected as a Commonwealth Fund fellow, which allowed me to complete a Masters in Public Health from the Harvard School of Public Health and learn more about Minority Health, Health disparities and health policy. It wasn't as if I particularly chose this route -- it honestly chose me. And I am glad that it did!

From there, I had a career as a family physician and Chief Medical Officer of the largest Federally Qualified Health Center system in Connecticut, where I was able to grow as a physician, medical executive and administrator, program developer, researcher and public health professional. My work led to greater visibility and subsequent recruitment to UCSF less than one year ago. So that, in a nutshell, is my life story. I hope you feel that I am worthy to make the assertions I offered earlier.

So back to why I told you medicine is not a job. Over the past few years, I have come to the firm and surprising realization that *medicine is not a job*. Though there are many reasons, some are beyond the scope of this book, but I will now tell you the top 5 reasons why I say this.

6
REASON NUMBER 5

Medicine is not a job reason number 5: Medicine is not a job because you are never "off duty". In most jobs, you have scheduled work hours and shifts, and when your shift is over, you are off duty. The average American worker does not go home and still work after they clock out.

Reason number 5: Medicine is not a job because you are never "off duty".

The average doctor never clocks out. You go home and think about the patients you took care of, look up things that may help them, and hope that they will be alive and well the next time you see them. You become the unofficial doctor for your parents, your family, your spouse, your kids, your church, the kid's soccer team or dance company, and even strangers in an airplane. If a patient calls you or needs you after hours, you respond, and you do it because….you just do it.

…you just do it.

Case in point:

Recently, my family and I made a long international trip to Singapore and other countries in Asia, and had a very busy, eventful and bustling trip. By the time we boarded the plane for a 17 hour trip back home, all we wanted to do on the plane was sleep and rest without disturbance. My kids fell asleep quickly and my husband shortly thereafter.

Just as I was about to finally doze off and enjoy the comfortable flight and uninterrupted sleep opportunity, I heard an overhead page – "If there is any doctor on board the plane, please press your call button for one of the flight attendants."

In that brief moment thousands of miles high in the sky, I debated on whether or not I should push the call button and wondered if anyone else would respond on the large Airbus. However, I knew that I had a responsibility to help, even though I was tired and exhausted, and even if there were other doctors that answered the call.

It was a good thing I pressed that call button. The flight attendant briefed me on a passenger in distress a few rows in front of us, and I went to go examine the man. Another woman had responded to the call, but was a Pediatric nurse who was licensed in another country, so was unable to provide the care he needed.

It was a good thing I pressed that call button.

I found a middle-aged, non-English speaking man in significant distress, complaining of sudden onset of severe right lower quadrant abdominal pain. Through the translation of his wife and daughter, I was able to get a history and understand their shock that this usually stoic and strong gentleman was now crying and miserable.

Though many things came to mind when I interviewed and examined him, I was very worried that he may have appendicitis, which would be serious. I worked with the passenger-turned-patient, the family and the flight crew to stabilize him and keep him comfortable, and to message the ground team that we would need an ambulance on arrival, which was still hours away.

After this, I could not sleep. I continued to check on the passenger-turned-patient, prayed that he would stabilize and not deteriorate during the remainder of the flight. The experience reminded me that medicine is not a job because you are never "off duty".

7
REASON NUMBER 4

Medicine is not a job reason number 4: Medicine is not a job because you don't get paid more for doing more. In many jobs, if you work longer, stay overtime, or do after-hours work, that translates into more pay.

Reason number 4: Medicine is not a job because you don't get paid more for doing more.

I am sorry to tell you that as a doctor, you will invest more in your work then you will ever get back, so welcome to the VIP membership level of overtime! Your overtime won't be considered, counted or compensated more, but you will do more and more for your patients because ...you just do it.

Case in point:

During my residency training, the national imperative to limit residents to the 80 hour workweek came to light. Prior to that, residents across the country were accustomed to working 120 hour weeks or more, getting very little sleep, and somehow managing to continue day after day.

When the 80 hour rule started, hospitals and training programs could face hefty and harsh fines for violating this rule. As residents, we would watch nursing shifts change, and entirely new teams come on the hospital floors in first, second, and third shifts.

One day in the Intensive Care Unit as junior resident, I had a very ill patient who was crashing and in multi-organ failure, and was requiring continuous monitoring. The nurse working with me was incredibly attentive and compassionate, and together we worked to keep the patient and his family at ease, giving them enough information on his situation without scaring them.

His wife and son told us we were a great team and they wanted us to remain assigned to the patient. I personally felt that I could not pass on this patient's care to anyone. When it was time for the nursing shift change, I asked the nurse if she could stay a few hours more so we could continue our caring partnership, and she told me that if she did so, she would have to get overtime pay for it, which required prior approval by her supervisor, so she would just sign the patient out to the night nurse.

I would not get paid more in dollars, but I would get more in satisfaction.

My nurse colleague was fantastic and gave a comprehensive signout, and the patient survived the night, but that was the first time I realized that <u>my</u> overtime was not being tracked, counted or paid, and that it was assumed given my role. No matter how long I stayed, how much more I did for this patient, and how much I deprived *myself of other things, I would not get paid more in dollars. Perhaps I would gain in satisfaction and peace. This experience taught me that medicine is not a job because you don't get paid more for doing more.*

8
REASON NUMBER 3

Medicine is not a job reason number 3: Medicine is not a job because it is immensely agonizing when things go wrong. Let's face it – things don't always go well in medicine. However, as the saying goes, "when things go wrong, you cannot go with them."

Reason number 3: Medicine is not a job because it is immensely agonizing when things go wrong.

You will work hard, study hard, plan hard, think hard and things may still not go as planned. People will still die at some point. Some medications will not work. People can do everything right and still get cancer. Kids will get terrible illnesses.

In many jobs, things go wrong and you can let them go. In medicine, you continue to think of what you could have done better, why you didn't do more, why you didn't do less, and you agonize over the unfortunate things that happen to patients because…you just do it.

Case in point:

I don't think any physician forgets their first patient death experience. Mine occurred with a young child who had a rare disease called Mucopolysaccharidosis Type I, a very rare metabolic disorder caused by the absence or malfunction of specific enzymes needed to break down long carbohydrates into forms we can use in our cells.

I don't think any physician forgets their first patient death experience.

This disease, also known as MPS, leads to neurological, respiratory, cognitive, ocular, cardiac and other physical impairments. My particular patient was about 4 years old and looked like he was less than 2 years old. He had multiple admissions for various upper and lower respiratory illnesses as well as bowel problems.

As I watched this child suffer during one particular admission for pneumonia, and his parents dote so much love and affection on him, my heart went out to them and I did my best to provide care for this child. Since he was my first patient who had this diagnosis and the only one I have seen in my career, I read a lot about the prognosis, complications and management of this condition. Unfortunately, on one particular admission for pneumonia, he had severe respiratory failure despite being ventilated, and he died one evening when I was on call, peacefully, according to his parents, who never left his side.

His parents were strong and resolved, but I was a wreck. I felt like I could have done more or should have been better. His parents consoled me and assuaged me, telling me I did all that I could and they had prepared for this day for a long time.

For the next few weeks, I continued to replay all

of my actions. I could not sleep or eat and I kicked myself for not knowing more about this rare disease. The experience affected every other dimension of my life.

I finally stopped agonizing and moved to a better place.

A few weeks later when I received a card from his parents and some pictures from his burial addressed to me as "the best doctor we have ever had," I finally stopped agonizing and moved to a better place. This experience reminded me that medicine is not a job, because it is immensely agonizing when things go wrong.

9
REASON NUMBER 2

Medicine is not a job reason number 2: Medicine is not a job because it is exceptionally rewarding when you get things right. Just as you agonize when things don't go well, you feel like a champion when things go right!

Reason number 2: Medicine is not a job because it is exceptionally rewarding when you get things right.

There is nothing more gratifying, rewarding or professionally satisfying that having a patient turn the corner , get their diabetes under control, deliver a healthy baby, come out successfully from a surgery, bounce out of a coma, or thank you for helping them through their depression. In many jobs, a thank you is almost expected – if you give something to someone in exchange for something, they usually say thank you – it is expected.

In medicine, the thanks often come from the healing and the joy of the patient and their family. Whether you are formally thanked or not, with your medical successes, you will continue to replay the steps that led to the success for that patient or that family because ...you just do it.

...thanks often come from the healing and joy of the patient and their family.

Case in point:

I will never forget a special patient of mine with poorly controlled diabetes who was suffering from many complications of his diabetes. He was warm, friendly, pleasant and patient. He also had a history of Hepatitis C and alcohol abuse in the past. As I took care of him and saw him back in the clinic for weekly visits, I titrated his insulin dose up, higher and higher, after he repeatedly got blood glucose values in the high 500s (or too high to be detected on the office glucometer/glucose machine).

I struggled to understand why his glucose values were not improving, and sometimes worsening, despite this medication management. One day, I called the pharmacist and inquired which dose of insulin was the last one he picked up, to which I was told that the patient had not obtained his insulin for months!

I was surprised and assumed he could not afford the costly medication, so I went to discuss his case with our access to care (ATC) worker, with the goal of finding affordable medication options for him. More than my surprise that he had not been filling his medications was my surprise to learn from the ATC worker that my patient was homeless!

On my next visit, I asked him more about this and he explained that he was homeless, estranged from his family, and living in his car. It was one of the saddest situations I experienced at the intersection of medicine and public health.

He could not obtain the insulin because he did not have a refrigerator to store it in. He was only able to go to the homeless shelter for a few hours at a time, and not every day.

It was one of the saddest situations I experienced at the intersection of medicine and public health.

I knew that I had to address his social issues before moving forward on any medical issues. Over the next few weeks, I wrote letters and opened a case with the City Housing Authority, urging them to find a safe housing option for my patient for medical reasons. About two months later, he was granted a small but furnished one bedroom apartment through a housing program for medically complex patients and he was on cloud 9!

A few months later, when the electric company threatened to shut off his electricity for lack of payment, I completed the paperwork attesting to his medical need for electricity and averting a shut off.

Slowly but surely, the patient and good health were finally acquainted. He was now able to make and keep appointments with other specialists to manage his diabetes complications. One day, after the Medical Assistant checked his Hemoglobin A1C, a measure of glucose control over the past few months, he ran into my exam room with excitement, in the middle of me seeing another patient, and exclaimed, "we did it! My A1C is 8.0!"

...the patient and good health were finally acquainted.

Prior to this, his A1C was 12, correlating to an average blood glucose of 300+, and it was now averaging under 200. He was on his way to excellent control and this was no small feat. We never had to use the higher doses of insulin I had prescribed months back because the stabilizing of his social situation empowered him to take control of his medical needs. I was so excited!

For days, and now years, I reflected on this story and the multiple implications for my practice, and could not contain my joy – I still tell anyone who will listen, just like you are! This experience reminded me that medicine is not a job, because it is exceptionally rewarding when you get things right.

10
REASON NUMBER 1

Medicine is not a job reason number 1: Medicine is not a job because you can never quit! In most jobs, you can quit if you don't like it. In medicine, you can't just quit.

Reason number 1: Medicine is not a job because you can never quit.

Even if you change jobs or diversify your work in medicine, you will always be a doctor and you will always think like one. You will consider problem-solving the way doctors think and you will always be prepared to respond to the call of duty, even when you are "off duty." You will go to war zones and conflict areas that no one wants to go to. You will rush to crisis areas after a car accident or a hurricane. You will be a doctor mom or doctor dad.

You will go to war zones and conflict areas that no one wants to go to.

Medicine will permeate every aspect of your life and you will respond as a doctor whenever it is needed because ....you just do it!

Case in point:

Any physician can relate to the S.O.A.P note thinking that pervades our lives. As medical students, we are trained to extract patient histories, conduct physical exams, write patient notes, transfer patients between providers and organize our thinking in what we call a S.O.A.P. note.

Any physician can related to the S.O.A.P. note thinking that pervades our lives.

*"S" is for **subjective** and descriptive parts of the patient's history – e.g. "I have had pain and swelling in my right leg for 6 days that comes and goes and started after a long airplane flight." "O" is for **objective** and physical findings on the patient's exam, appearance and diagnostic studies – e.g. "the patient's right leg is tender and swollen along the calf and the patient has a positive Homan's sign suggestive of a deep venous thrombosis (blood clot)," or, "the ultrasound of the lower leg confirms the clinical suspicion of a DVT."*

*"A" is for the **assessment**, where physician sleuthing emerges. In "A," we summarize the patient and create our differential diagnosis for the presenting symptom, and then use "S" and "O" to narrow the differential. For example: "The differential diagnosis of right leg pain and swelling includes trauma, musculoskeletal causes, cellulitis, DVT, rhabdomyolysis, a muscle disorder, etc. Based on the clinical findings and*

history and the temporal relationship to the long airplane ride and hormone replacement therapy that predisposed her to venous stasis, my assessment is that she has a DVT."

*The "P" is for the **plan**, which is where we outline the treatment and management in partnership with the patient. It is at this point where we say what we are going to do, e.g. "I will start the patient on heparin followed by warfarin and this will require close monitoring and dietary restrictions."*

A friend of mine left the medical field in mid-career to go into the banking industry, feeling quite jaded with her practice. She told me that one day, one of the tellers in her bank came up short when they were counting money in the registers for the day. After counting and recounting the teller's drawer, and coming up short, she decided to help her team address the problem in SOAP style.

Through this process, they came up with a short "differential" of what could have happened and finally realized that the teller had given one patient a $10 bill instead of a $5 bill on one transaction. But in that process, she realized she could never, even in another industry, stop thinking like a doctor. "Who am I kidding?" she said. "Once a doctor, always a doctor."

She has since returned to medicine in a practice setting that is more conducive to her skills and personality. This experience reminded me that medicine is not a job, because you can never quit.

"Who am I kidding? Once a doctor, always a doctor."

11
WHAT'S THE POINT?

So, if medicine is not a job, what is it? As altruistic as it sounds, I believe that medicine is a calling. It takes a certain amount of inexplicable, unnatural heart to spend the time, energy, money and passion to enter a field that does not guarantee you a job.

Medicine is a calling.

It takes a lot to go through medical training and enter the medical workforce knowing that you will never be off duty, you won't get paid more for doing more, you will agonize over tough situations, you will be unusually happy about good results, and you can never quit.

Despite all of this, going into medicine was the best decision I have ever made. I won't say I have not made mistakes – I have. But I have learned and grown from them and my mistakes have made me more convicted in my learning process. And though it is sometimes intellectually challenging and physically exhausting, I love taking care of patients and learning from them. That is the sign of a calling.

Going into medicine was the best decision I have ever made.

I have been able to have a very rich and diverse career in medicine so far – delivering care, studying how care is delivered, advocating for better care and teaching learners how to deliver care.

I have been fortunate to have great mentors and advisors who helped me answer the call and helped me realize why I couldn't quit when I had sleepless nights, tough exams in college, long shifts or rough days, why I could not turn my pager off even though I was post call, why I took so many standardized exams and still take them now, or why I spent hours trying to figure out what could cause a complex myriad of symptoms.

There are so many points on the pathway to becoming a physician and practicing as a physician where you could easily throw in the towel. But it has been pretty much impossible for me, and many of my colleagues, to do so!

12
AND FINALLY!

I hope this short book encourages you and lets you know that I congratulate you for answering the call to go into medicine or the call to stay in medicine. As I said, the fact that you bought, or even better, read this book says a lot already.

I congratulate you for answering the call to go into medicine or the call to stay in medicine.

Maybe you are contemplating a career in medicine as you are in middle school or high school and you want to know what it looks like. Maybe you are in college or a post-baccalaureate in the process of applying to medical school or preparing for your first, second or third MCAT.

Maybe you are in medical school and trying to master anatomy, physiology and pathology late at night. Perhaps you are a medical student on clinical rotations wondering when you will ever be as smart as the residents. Maybe you are a resident physician wondering when you will get a good night's sleep and a wholesome dinner. Or maybe you are a practicing physician overwhelmed by the complexity of delivering health care safely and efficiently with high quality. It does not matter who you are and where in the pipeline you are. You read this book for a reason and you have a call to respond to.

You read this book for a reason and you have a call to respond to.

When it seems like you are missing all of the fun

studying for the SATs, volunteering in a hospital, doing a summer research programs, taking extra credit or AP classes, staying up late, waking up early, studying for the MCAT, USMLE Step 1, 2 or 3, the specialty boards or recertification, just remember what you read!

I hope you are not doing this because you want to get a job or keep a job. I hope you are doing this because you are responding to a calling. Rajesh Setty, a famous thinker and entrepreneur has said this about callings: "when your calling calls you, make sure that it does not get a busy signal!"

"When your calling calls you, make sure that it does not get a busy signal!"

Keep calm, stay in the race, keep up the good work, and I promise you.....when you finish running this race, you will definitely be employed! I don't know you personally, but I know you will be hired or re-hired! It may be cliché to end this book with "Confucius says," but I leave you with this famous quote by Confucius:

MEDICINE IS NOT A JOB!

"Choose a job you love and you will never have to work a day in your life." Here's to your stellar journey to a jobless, non-working, professionally gratifying medical career!

"Choose a job you love and you will never have to work a day in your life."

ABOUT THE AUTHOR

Dr. Olayiwola, also known as @DrNwando, is a family physician, primary care leader, researcher, innovator and educator. She is currently the Associate Director of the Center for Excellence in Primary Care and an Assistant Professor in the Department of Family and Community Medicine at University of California, San Francisco.

She is also a wife and a mother of two young children. She is a highly acclaimed speaker, writer and health care leader, and she passionately enjoys educating and mentoring students and professionals across the globe.

www.ingramcontent.com/pod-product-compliance
Lightning Source LLC
Chambersburg PA
CBHW061300040426
42444CB00010B/2443